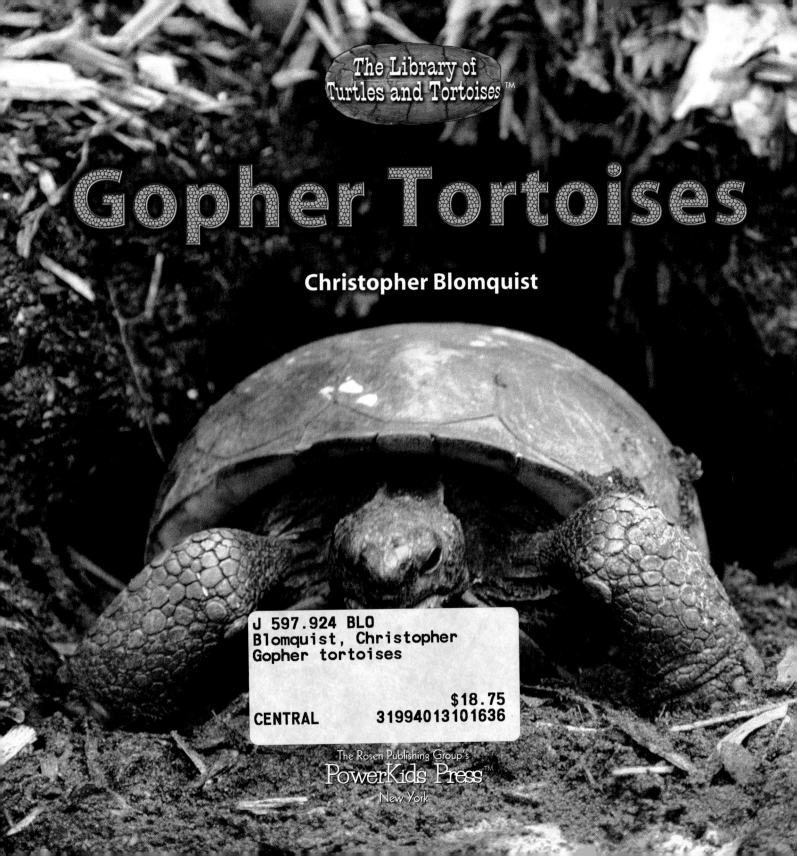

The Library of Turtles and Tortoises™

Gopher Tortoises

Christopher Blomquist

The Rosen Publishing Group's
PowerKids Press™
New York

For Carolyn, a friend to kith and creatures

Published in 2004 by The Rosen Publishing Group, Inc.
29 East 21st Street, New York, NY 10010

First Edition

Editor: Natashya Wilson
Book Design: Michael J. Caroleo

Photo Credits: Cover, title page, pp. 12, 15 © Index Stock Imagery; p. 4 © Fred Whitehead/Animals Animals; p. 7 (top left) © George Huey/Animals Animals; p. 7 (top and bottom right) © Dennis Sheridan; pp. 7 (bottom left), 16 © Tony Arruza/CORBIS; p. 8 © Doug Wechsler/Animals Animals; p. 11 © Philip Hart/Animals Animals; p. 19 © John Pontier/Animals Animals; p. 20 (top) © Kennan Ward/CORBIS; p. 20 (bottom) © Lynda Richardson/CORBIS.

Blomquist, Christopher.
Gopher tortoises / Christopher Blomquist.— 1st ed.
    p. cm. — (The library of turtles and tortoises)
Summary: Nature's bulldozer — The name game — Size and shape — Homes on the range — A fresh meal of plants — The mating dance — Baby beware! — To hibernate or not to hibernate? — Dangers new and old — Protecting desert tortoises.
Includes bibliographical references (p.   ).
ISBN 0-8239-6740-9 (lib. bdg.)
1. Gopher tortoise—Juvenile literature. [1. Gopher tortoise. 2. Turtles.] I. Title. II. Series.
QL666.C584 B66 2004
597.92'4—dc21
                              2002155839

Manufactured in the United States of America

Contents

Turtle and Tortoise Facts

Gopher tortoises help their habitat in two ways. Their digging brings nutrients to the surface of the soil, and they spread plant seeds in their solid waste. Both of these things help new plants to grow.

Gopher Tortoise Homes in the United States

Nature's Bulldozer

Gopher tortoises live in sandy, grassy areas of South Carolina, Georgia, Florida, Louisiana, Mississippi, and Alabama. They get their name because they dig underground **burrows**, as do gophers. An average gopher tortoise burrow is large. It can be 35 feet (10 m) long and can go as deep as 10 feet (3 m) under ground. Gopher tortoises have broad, flat front legs with long claws, made for digging. These shovel-like legs allow the gopher tortoise to move dirt easily, as does a bulldozer.

Gopher tortoise burrows provide homes for other animals, too. More than 300 kinds of insects and 50 different **vertebrates**, such as mice, snakes, and lizards, live with gopher tortoises in these roomy tunnels. If the tortoises weren't around to dig burrows, these **species** might die out.

This view shows a gopher tortoise in its burrow. The end of the burrow is just big enough for the tortoise to turn around.

The Name Game

Gopher tortoises have a number of names. Many people call them gophers for short. All tortoises, including gophers, are turtles. However, tortoises are **terrestrial**, or land-dwelling, turtles. They drink water and sometimes swim in it, but they don't live in water, as do many other turtles. A tortoise's shell is also higher and more dome shaped than are most other turtles' shells. Tortoises also have round, flat-bottomed hind feet that look like elephants' feet. A tortoise's feet are never webbed.

Gopher tortoises are one of four different species of tortoises that live in North America. The others are the desert, the Texas, and the Bolson tortoises. Scientists believe that tortoises have been on Earth for more than 60 million years.

North American tortoises include the Bolson tortoise (top left), *which lives only in Mexico, the gopher tortoise* (bottom left), *the desert tortoise* (bottom right), *and the Texas tortoise* (top right).

Turtle and Tortoise Facts

Tortoises are famous for being slow-moving creatures. Gopher tortoises walk at speeds of about $\frac{1}{10}$ to $\frac{3}{10}$ miles per hour (.2–.5 km/h).

Carapace

Plastron

Size and Shape

How can you tell if a tortoise is a gopher tortoise? Adult gopher tortoises are usually about 12 inches (30.4 cm) long and weigh from 9 to 15 pounds (4.1–6.8 kg). The largest gopher tortoise ever found was 15 inches (38.1 cm) long. Compared to other tortoises, gopher tortoises have wider heads, smaller back feet, and longer shells. The top half of the shell, called the **carapace**, is brown or tan. The **plastron**, or part of the shell that covers the tortoise's belly, is yellow. An adult female gopher's plastron is perfectly flat. A male's is slightly dented, like a spoon. This is the easiest way to tell female gophers and male gophers apart. A gopher tortoise cannot close itself inside its shell. Instead, gophers draw in their heads and block their shell openings with their front legs when they sense danger.

This gopher tortoise guards itself from danger by pulling in its head and using its scaly front legs as a wall.

Homes on the Range

Gopher tortoises use their flat front legs to dig their burrows. The long, deep tunnels are wide enough at the end for the tortoise to turn around inside. A gopher burrow has just one opening. The top of the burrow is rounded. The earth around the entrance is called the apron.

An adult gopher tortoise may dig several burrows in its **home range**. A home range can be as large as 8 acres (3.2 ha), though most are smaller. In one part of Florida, males use an average of 17 burrows each and females use an average of 9 burrows. The tortoises move back and forth between burrows. Although two gophers sometimes share a burrow, there is usually just one tortoise per burrow. Scientists don't know what causes gopher tortoises to switch burrows or to dig new ones.

Most gopher tortoises, such as this one, dig their burrows in the sandy soil of grassy areas on the edge of forests.

A Fresh Meal of Plants

Gopher tortoises are mostly **herbivores**, or plant-eating animals. Their favorite foods include grasses, flowers, fruits, vegetables, and mushrooms. Sometimes gopher tortoises eat **dung** or pieces of bone. Their bodies need the vitamins and other nutrients found in those things. Like all turtles, gophers do not have teeth. The hard, bony plates that form their beaklike mouths are sharp enough to chop up food.

As cold-blooded **reptiles**, tortoises do not have a constant body **temperature**. Sunlight and air temperature can change a tortoise's body temperature. This affects how active the tortoise is. **Nutrients** in certain plants can help a tortoise to steady its body temperature. This may be why gophers eat certain foods at certain times.

Gopher tortoises eat a lot of grass. Gophers usually stay close to the entrances of their burrows when eating.

The Mating Dance

Gopher tortoises **mate** in the spring and the summer, during April, May, and June. During mating season, a male will look for a mate by visiting the burrows of at least two females. He may also make raspy sounds to attract females. When a male gopher finds a mate, he walks in circles and bobs his head up and down. He then bites her legs before he mates with her.

The female is ready to lay her eggs a few days after mating. She digs a nest that is about 6 inches (15.2 cm) deep and lays from 1 to 25 eggs. Then she covers them with soil. Unlike many other turtle species, gopher tortoises produce just one **clutch** of eggs per year. Once a mother turtle buries her eggs, she has nothing more to do with the nest or the babies.

Here a male gopher tortoise (right) is courting a female gopher tortoise (left). Sometimes two or three males court the same female.

Turtle and Tortoise Facts

Tortoises do not have ears outside their heads. They do have a kind of inner ear, but they probably do most of their hearing by picking up vibrations, or rapid movements, from the ground.

Baby Beware!

Gopher tortoise eggs take different amounts of time to hatch. Often, the **incubation** time depends on where the nest is located. In Georgia, it may take 100 days for the babies, called **hatchlings**, to appear. In Florida, where it is usually a bit warmer, the eggs may need only from 80 to 90 days to incubate. Gopher hatchlings are orange and are about 2 inches (5 cm) long. Their color darkens as they get older. When they are from 10 to 21 years old, they start having babies of their own. However, only 2 or 3 of every 100 will live more than 2 years. Many eggs never hatch at all because they are eaten by **predators** such as skunks, raccoons, snakes, and fire ants. Hatchlings will hide under plants or in burrows for safety. They are easy **prey** until they are 6 or 7 years old.

A gopher tortoise hatchling fits in the palm of a human hand. Once hatchlings are born, they must take care of themselves.

To Hibernate or Not to Hibernate?

Many gopher tortoises live through cold weather by **hibernating**, or going to sleep for the winter. Whether or not an individual gopher will do this depends on where it lives. Gophers in central and southern Florida are active all year long. They may stay in their burrows on cooler days, but usually they do not hibernate. Gophers in South Carolina will hibernate during the winter months and will awaken in the spring, when more plants grow.

Gopher tortoises also become less active if the weather is really hot. During the summer, gophers may come out of their burrows only in the mornings and the evenings, when the air is cooler. The burrow stays about the same temperature and has the same wetness, no matter what the temperature is outside. This is called a **microhabitat**.

A gopher tortoise's burrow offers it shelter from both the cold of winter and the heat of summer.

Turtle and Tortoise Facts

Wildfires can be good for gopher tortoises. The fires open up overgrown areas to the sun and let new, juicy plants grow there.

Dangers Old and New

Gopher tortoises can live from 40 to 60 years. However, many of them do not live that long. Predators such as dogs and coyotes will attack adult gopher tortoises. They may hurt the gophers, but usually the tortoises' hard shells keep them from being killed. People are a greater danger to gophers. Gophers that crawl onto roads can be killed by cars. In many places, buildings have ruined the gophers' natural **habitat**. Years ago, people ate gopher tortoise meat. Ancient peoples used gopher tortoise shells for pots and bowls. People also used to catch gophers and hold tortoise races. Fake gopher tortoises are now used for the races. Today hunting gopher tortoises is illegal in most states.

Top: *Coyotes will attack gopher tortoises.* Bottom: *Male gophers sometimes tip each other over in a fight. The tipped tortoise uses its head and legs to right itself, as this tortoise is doing. If a tortoise tips over and cannot right itself, it will die.*

Protecting Gopher Tortoises

People now know how important the gopher tortoise is to the natural world. Many states have passed laws to protect the gophers. In Florida, it is illegal to harm, kill, catch, move, or even feed a tortoise without a permit. This law also prevents people from keeping these animals as pets. However, laws cannot keep all the gophers safe. Governments can and do grant permits that allow builders to clear wild land and build on it.

Today people sometimes find gopher tortoises living in their yards. If you are lucky enough to see a gopher tortoise in the wild or to have one living near you, enjoy watching the turtle from afar, but be careful to leave it alone. Like the insects, snakes, and other creatures that share the gopher tortoise's burrow, humans can learn to live peacefully near the deep-digging gopher tortoise, too!

Glossary

burrows (BUR-ohz) Holes animals dig in the ground for shelter.

carapace (KER-uh-pays) The upper part of a turtle's shell.

clutch (KLUCH) The eggs laid by a female tortoise at one time.

dung (DUNG) Animal waste.

habitat (HA-bih-tat) The surroundings where an animal or a plant naturally lives.

hatchlings (HACH-lingz) Baby animals that have just come out of their eggs.

herbivores (ER-bih-vorz) Animals that eat plants.

hibernating (HY-bur-nayt-ing) Spending the winter in a sleeplike state.

home range (HOHM RAYNJ) The area in which an animal usually stays.

incubation (in-kyoo-BAY-shun) The time it takes for an egg to hatch.

mate (MAYT) To join together to make babies.

microhabitat (my-kroh-HA-bih-tat) A small area, in which animals live, that is different from the other surroundings.

nutrients (NOO-tree-ints) Food parts that living things need to live and to grow.

plastron (PLAS-tron) The bottom, flatter part of a tortoise's shell that covers the belly.

predators (PREH-duh-terz) Animals that hunt other animals for food.

prey (PRAY) Animals that are hunted by other animals for food.

reptiles (REP-tylz) A group of cold-blooded animals with lungs and scales, such as turtles, snakes, and lizards.

species (SPEE-sheez) A single kind of living thing. All humans are one species.

temperature (TEM-pruh-cher) How hot or cold something is.

terrestrial (teh-RES-tree-ul) Living on land, not in the air or water.

vertebrates (VER-tih-brits) Animals that have backbones.

Index

A
apron, 10

B
Bolson tortoise, 6
burrow(s), 5, 10, 14,
    18

C
carapace, 9
clutch, 14

D
desert tortoise, 6

E
eggs, 14, 17

F
Florida, 5, 10, 17–18,
    22
food, 13

H
hatchlings, 17
herbivores, 13
hibernating, 18
home range, 10

M
mate, 14
microhabitat, 18

P
plastron, 9
predators, 17, 21
prey, 17

S
shell(s), 6, 9, 21

T
temperature, 13
Texas tortoise, 6

Web Sites

Due to the changing nature of Internet links, PowerKids Press has developed an online list of Web sites related to the subject of this book. This site is updated regularly. Please use this link to access the list:
www.powerkidslinks.com/ltt/gopher/